50 Canada Recipes for Home

By: Kelly Johnson

Table of Contents

- Maple-glazed salmon
- Poutine
- Butter tarts
- Nanaimo bars
- Tourtière
- Bannock
- BeaverTails
- Lobster roll
- Saskatoon berry pie
- Montreal bagels
- Nova Scotia seafood chowder
- Montreal smoked meat sandwich
- Alberta beef steak
- Pacific salmon with maple glaze
- Newfoundland cod au gratin
- Blueberry grunt
- Montreal-style bagels with smoked salmon
- Butter chicken poutine
- Quebecois meat pie (tourtière du Lac-Saint-Jean)
- Haddock and chips
- Timbits
- Saskatoon berry muffins
- Maple-glazed donuts
- Elk burgers
- Wild rice pilaf
- Atlantic lobster bisque
- PEI potato scallops
- Nova Scotia blueberry grunt
- Butter tart squares
- Pemmican
- Quebecois pea soup (soupe aux pois)
- Montreal-style steak seasoning
- Maritime seafood boil
- Canadian bacon and pineapple pizza
- Alberta beef chili

- Maple syrup bacon-wrapped scallops
- Haskap berry jam
- Newfoundland toutons with molasses
- Arctic char with dill sauce
- Butter tart ice cream
- Canadian whisky cocktails
- Quebecois sugar pie (tarte au sucre)
- Pacific oysters Rockefeller
- Prairie oysters (bull testicles)
- Maple-glazed pork chops
- Atlantic salmon burgers
- Moose stew
- Blueberry pancakes with maple syrup
- Caribou steaks
- Nanaimo bar cheesecake

Maple-glazed salmon

Ingredients:

- 4 salmon fillets (about 6 ounces each), skin-on
- Salt and pepper, to taste
- 1/4 cup maple syrup
- 2 tablespoons soy sauce
- 1 tablespoon Dijon mustard
- 1 tablespoon olive oil
- 2 cloves garlic, minced
- 1 teaspoon grated fresh ginger
- 1 tablespoon chopped fresh parsley (optional, for garnish)

Instructions:

1. Preheat your oven to 400°F (200°C). Line a baking sheet with parchment paper or lightly grease it with oil.
2. Season the salmon fillets with salt and pepper on both sides, then place them skin-side down on the prepared baking sheet.
3. In a small bowl, whisk together the maple syrup, soy sauce, Dijon mustard, olive oil, minced garlic, and grated ginger until well combined.
4. Pour the maple syrup mixture evenly over the salmon fillets, making sure they are well coated.
5. Place the baking sheet in the preheated oven and bake for 12-15 minutes, or until the salmon is cooked through and flakes easily with a fork.
6. If desired, broil the salmon for an additional 1-2 minutes at the end to caramelize the glaze slightly.
7. Remove the salmon from the oven and let it rest for a few minutes before serving.
8. Garnish with chopped fresh parsley, if desired, and serve the maple-glazed salmon hot.

This Maple-Glazed Salmon is perfect served with your favorite sides, such as roasted vegetables, rice, or salad, for a delicious and nutritious meal. Enjoy!

Poutine

Ingredients:

- 4 large potatoes, peeled and cut into fries
- Vegetable oil, for frying
- 2 cups cheese curds
- 2 cups beef gravy (homemade or store-bought)
- Salt, to taste
- Fresh chopped parsley (optional, for garnish)

Instructions:

1. Start by making the French fries. Rinse the cut potatoes under cold water to remove excess starch. Pat them dry with paper towels.
2. Heat vegetable oil in a deep fryer or large pot to 325°F (160°C). Fry the potatoes in batches until golden brown and crispy, about 5-7 minutes per batch. Remove the fries from the oil and drain them on paper towels. Allow them to cool slightly.
3. While the fries are still warm, season them with salt to taste.
4. In a separate saucepan, heat the beef gravy over medium heat until warmed through. Keep it warm while you assemble the poutine.
5. To assemble the poutine, place a generous portion of French fries on a serving plate or in a bowl.
6. Sprinkle cheese curds over the hot fries, ensuring they are evenly distributed.
7. Pour the warm gravy over the fries and cheese curds, making sure to cover them completely.
8. Garnish with fresh chopped parsley, if desired, for added flavor and color.
9. Serve the poutine immediately while hot, allowing the cheese curds to melt slightly from the warmth of the gravy.

Enjoy your homemade poutine as a comforting and indulgent treat, perfect for sharing with friends or enjoying as a satisfying snack!

Butter tarts

Ingredients:

For the pastry:

- 1 and 1/4 cups all-purpose flour
- 1/4 teaspoon salt
- 1/2 cup cold unsalted butter, cut into small cubes
- 1/4 cup ice water

For the filling:

- 1/2 cup packed brown sugar
- 1/2 cup corn syrup or maple syrup
- 1/4 cup unsalted butter, melted
- 1 large egg
- 1 teaspoon vanilla extract
- 1/4 cup raisins or chopped pecans (optional)

Instructions:

1. Start by making the pastry. In a large mixing bowl, combine the flour and salt. Add the cold butter cubes and use a pastry cutter or fork to cut the butter into the flour until the mixture resembles coarse crumbs.
2. Gradually add the ice water, a tablespoon at a time, mixing with a fork until the dough comes together. Be careful not to overwork the dough.
3. Shape the dough into a disk, wrap it in plastic wrap, and refrigerate for at least 30 minutes to chill.
4. Preheat your oven to 375°F (190°C). Lightly grease a muffin tin or line it with paper liners.
5. On a lightly floured surface, roll out the chilled pastry dough to about 1/8 inch thickness. Use a round cutter or glass to cut out circles slightly larger than the muffin tin openings.
6. Gently press the pastry circles into the prepared muffin tin, forming shallow cups. Trim any excess dough from the edges.
7. In a medium mixing bowl, whisk together the brown sugar, corn syrup or maple syrup, melted butter, egg, and vanilla extract until smooth.

8. If using, distribute the raisins or chopped pecans evenly among the pastry-lined muffin tins.
9. Carefully pour the filling mixture into each pastry cup, filling them about 3/4 full.
10. Bake in the preheated oven for 15-18 minutes, or until the pastry is golden brown and the filling is set but still slightly jiggly in the center.
11. Remove from the oven and let the butter tarts cool in the muffin tin for a few minutes before transferring them to a wire rack to cool completely.
12. Once cooled, serve the butter tarts at room temperature and enjoy!

These homemade butter tarts are sure to be a hit with their deliciously sweet and gooey filling encased in a flaky pastry crust.

Nanaimo bars

Ingredients:

For the base:

- 1/2 cup unsalted butter, melted
- 1/4 cup granulated sugar
- 5 tablespoons cocoa powder
- 1 large egg, beaten
- 1 and 3/4 cups graham cracker crumbs
- 1 cup shredded coconut
- 1/2 cup chopped nuts (walnuts or almonds)

For the middle layer:

- 1/2 cup unsalted butter, softened
- 2 cups powdered sugar
- 2 tablespoons vanilla custard powder (such as Bird's)
- 2 tablespoons milk or cream

For the top layer:

- 4 ounces semi-sweet chocolate, chopped
- 2 tablespoons unsalted butter

Instructions:

1. Line an 8x8-inch baking dish with parchment paper, leaving some overhang on the sides for easy removal later.
2. In a medium saucepan, melt 1/2 cup of butter over low heat. Stir in the granulated sugar and cocoa powder until smooth.
3. Remove the saucepan from the heat and gradually whisk in the beaten egg until well combined. Return the saucepan to low heat and cook, stirring constantly, for 1-2 minutes until slightly thickened.
4. Remove the saucepan from the heat and stir in the graham cracker crumbs, shredded coconut, and chopped nuts until evenly combined.

5. Press the mixture firmly and evenly into the bottom of the prepared baking dish. Place the dish in the refrigerator while you prepare the middle layer.
6. In a mixing bowl, beat together 1/2 cup of softened butter, powdered sugar, vanilla custard powder, and milk or cream until smooth and creamy.
7. Spread the custard mixture evenly over the chilled base layer in the baking dish. Return the dish to the refrigerator while you prepare the top layer.
8. In a heatproof bowl set over a pot of simmering water, melt the chopped chocolate and 2 tablespoons of butter together, stirring until smooth.
9. Pour the melted chocolate mixture over the chilled custard layer and spread it out evenly with a spatula.
10. Return the dish to the refrigerator and chill for at least 2 hours, or until the Nanaimo bars are set.
11. Once set, use the parchment paper overhang to lift the bars out of the baking dish. Place them on a cutting board and cut into squares or bars.
12. Serve and enjoy! Store any leftover Nanaimo bars in an airtight container in the refrigerator for up to one week.

These homemade Nanaimo bars are sure to impress with their irresistible combination of flavors and textures!

Tourtière

Ingredients:

For the pastry:

- 2 and 1/2 cups all-purpose flour
- 1 cup cold unsalted butter, cut into small cubes
- 1 teaspoon salt
- 1/4 to 1/2 cup ice water

For the filling:

- 1 lb ground pork
- 1/2 lb ground beef
- 1 onion, finely chopped
- 2 cloves garlic, minced
- 1/2 teaspoon ground cinnamon
- 1/4 teaspoon ground cloves
- 1/4 teaspoon ground nutmeg
- Salt and pepper, to taste
- 1/2 cup beef or chicken broth
- 1/4 cup breadcrumbs (optional, for binding)

Instructions:

1. To make the pastry, in a large mixing bowl, combine the flour and salt. Add the cold butter cubes and use a pastry cutter or your fingertips to work the butter into the flour until the mixture resembles coarse crumbs.
2. Gradually add the ice water, a little at a time, mixing with a fork until the dough comes together. Be careful not to overwork the dough. Shape the dough into a disc, wrap it in plastic wrap, and refrigerate for at least 30 minutes.
3. In a large skillet or frying pan, cook the ground pork and beef over medium heat until browned and cooked through, breaking it up with a spoon as it cooks.
4. Add the chopped onion and minced garlic to the skillet with the cooked meat and cook for an additional 3-4 minutes until the onion is softened.
5. Stir in the ground cinnamon, ground cloves, ground nutmeg, salt, and pepper, to taste. Cook for another minute to allow the spices to become fragrant.

6. Pour in the beef or chicken broth and bring the mixture to a simmer. Let it cook for 5-7 minutes until most of the liquid has evaporated. If the mixture seems too wet, you can stir in the breadcrumbs to help bind the filling.
7. Preheat your oven to 375°F (190°C). Lightly grease a 9-inch pie dish.
8. Roll out half of the chilled pastry dough on a lightly floured surface to fit the bottom of the pie dish. Place it in the bottom of the dish and press it down gently to fit. Trim any excess dough from the edges.
9. Spoon the cooked meat mixture evenly into the pastry-lined pie dish, spreading it out into an even layer.
10. Roll out the remaining pastry dough on a lightly floured surface to fit the top of the pie. Place it over the filling and crimp the edges to seal. Cut a few slits in the top crust to allow steam to escape during baking.
11. Bake the tourtière in the preheated oven for 45-50 minutes, or until the crust is golden brown and the filling is heated through.
12. Remove the tourtière from the oven and let it cool for a few minutes before slicing and serving.

Enjoy your homemade tourtière warm, with a side of cranberry sauce or your favorite condiments, for a comforting and festive meal!

Bannock

Ingredients:

- 2 cups all-purpose flour
- 2 teaspoons baking powder
- 1/2 teaspoon salt
- 1 tablespoon sugar (optional)
- 2 tablespoons butter or vegetable oil
- 3/4 cup water or milk (approximately)
- Additional flour for dusting

Instructions:

1. In a large mixing bowl, whisk together the flour, baking powder, salt, and sugar (if using) until well combined.
2. Cut the butter into small pieces and add it to the dry ingredients. Use your fingers or a pastry cutter to rub the butter into the flour mixture until it resembles coarse crumbs.
3. Gradually add the water or milk, a little at a time, stirring with a wooden spoon or your hands, until a soft dough forms. You may not need to use all of the liquid, so add it gradually until the dough comes together.
4. Turn the dough out onto a lightly floured surface and knead it gently for a few minutes until smooth and elastic. If the dough is too sticky, you can add a little more flour as needed.
5. Shape the dough into a round disc, about 1/2 inch thick.
6. Heat a lightly greased skillet or griddle over medium heat. Once hot, carefully transfer the bannock dough to the skillet.
7. Cook the bannock for 5-7 minutes on each side, or until golden brown and cooked through. You can cover the skillet with a lid to help the bannock cook evenly.
8. Alternatively, you can bake the bannock in a preheated oven at 375°F (190°C) for 20-25 minutes, or until golden brown and cooked through.
9. Once cooked, remove the bannock from the skillet or oven and let it cool slightly before slicing and serving.

Enjoy your freshly baked bannock warm, with butter, jam, honey, or your favorite toppings. It's perfect for breakfast, lunch, or as a side dish with soups and stews!

BeaverTails

Ingredients:

For the dough:

- 1 package (2 and 1/4 teaspoons) active dry yeast
- 1 cup warm water (about 110°F/45°C)
- 1/4 cup granulated sugar
- 1/4 cup unsalted butter, melted
- 1 teaspoon salt
- 3 to 3 and 1/2 cups all-purpose flour

For frying and topping:

- Vegetable oil, for frying
- Granulated sugar or cinnamon sugar, for dusting
- Optional toppings: Nutella, peanut butter, chocolate sauce, caramel sauce, whipped cream, crushed cookies, chopped nuts, sprinkles, etc.

Instructions:

1. In a small bowl, combine the warm water and sugar. Sprinkle the yeast over the mixture and let it sit for about 5-10 minutes, or until foamy.
2. In a large mixing bowl, combine the melted butter, salt, and 2 cups of flour. Add the yeast mixture and stir until well combined.
3. Gradually add enough of the remaining flour, 1/2 cup at a time, until the dough comes together and pulls away from the sides of the bowl.
4. Turn the dough out onto a lightly floured surface and knead it for about 5-7 minutes, or until it is smooth and elastic.
5. Place the dough in a greased bowl, cover it with a clean kitchen towel or plastic wrap, and let it rise in a warm, draft-free place for about 1 hour, or until doubled in size.
6. Punch down the risen dough and divide it into 8 equal portions. Shape each portion into an oval or elongated shape, about 1/4 inch thick.
7. Heat vegetable oil in a deep fryer or large pot to 375°F (190°C). Carefully fry the BeaverTails, one or two at a time, until golden brown and crispy, about 2-3 minutes per side.

8. Remove the fried BeaverTails from the oil using a slotted spoon and drain them on paper towels to remove excess oil.
9. While still warm, sprinkle the BeaverTails generously with granulated sugar or cinnamon sugar.
10. If desired, top the BeaverTails with your favorite toppings, such as Nutella, peanut butter, chocolate sauce, caramel sauce, whipped cream, crushed cookies, chopped nuts, or sprinkles.
11. Serve the BeaverTails warm and enjoy!

These homemade BeaverTails are sure to be a hit with their crispy exterior and deliciously sweet toppings. Customize them with your favorite flavors for a fun and indulgent treat!

Lobster roll

Ingredients:

- 1 and 1/2 pounds cooked lobster meat, chopped into bite-sized pieces
- 1/2 cup mayonnaise
- 2 celery stalks, finely diced
- 2 green onions, thinly sliced
- 1 tablespoon lemon juice
- Salt and pepper, to taste
- 4 split-top hot dog buns
- 2 tablespoons unsalted butter, melted
- Chopped fresh parsley, for garnish (optional)

Instructions:

1. In a large mixing bowl, combine the chopped lobster meat, mayonnaise, diced celery, sliced green onions, and lemon juice. Stir until well combined.
2. Season the lobster mixture with salt and pepper to taste. Adjust the seasoning as needed.
3. Heat a skillet or griddle over medium heat. Brush the split-top hot dog buns with melted butter on the outsides.
4. Place the buttered buns on the skillet or griddle, buttered side down, and cook until lightly toasted and golden brown, about 1-2 minutes.
5. Remove the toasted buns from the skillet and fill each with a generous portion of the lobster mixture.
6. Garnish the lobster rolls with chopped fresh parsley, if desired.
7. Serve the lobster rolls immediately, accompanied by your favorite side dishes, such as potato chips, coleslaw, or a green salad.

Enjoy these delicious lobster rolls as a summertime treat or as a special meal any time of the year!

Saskatoon berry pie

Ingredients:

For the pie crust:

- 2 and 1/2 cups all-purpose flour
- 1 teaspoon salt
- 1 cup cold unsalted butter, cut into small cubes
- 6-8 tablespoons ice water

For the filling:

- 5 cups Saskatoon berries, fresh or frozen
- 3/4 cup granulated sugar
- 1/4 cup all-purpose flour
- 1 tablespoon lemon juice
- 1/2 teaspoon ground cinnamon (optional)
- 1/4 teaspoon ground nutmeg (optional)
- 2 tablespoons unsalted butter, cut into small cubes

For assembly:

- 1 egg, beaten (for egg wash)
- 1 tablespoon granulated sugar (for sprinkling)

Instructions:

1. Preheat your oven to 375°F (190°C). Grease a 9-inch pie dish and set aside.
2. In a large mixing bowl, whisk together the flour and salt for the pie crust. Add the cold butter cubes and use a pastry cutter or your fingertips to work the butter into the flour until the mixture resembles coarse crumbs.
3. Gradually add the ice water, 1 tablespoon at a time, mixing with a fork until the dough just comes together. Be careful not to overwork the dough. Shape the dough into two equal-sized discs, wrap each in plastic wrap, and refrigerate for at least 30 minutes.

4. In a separate mixing bowl, combine the Saskatoon berries, granulated sugar, flour, lemon juice, ground cinnamon (if using), and ground nutmeg (if using). Toss until the berries are evenly coated.
5. Roll out one disc of the chilled pie dough on a lightly floured surface to fit the bottom of the prepared pie dish. Carefully transfer the rolled-out dough to the pie dish and press it gently into the bottom and sides.
6. Pour the Saskatoon berry filling into the prepared pie crust, spreading it out evenly. Dot the top of the filling with the cubed butter.
7. Roll out the second disc of chilled pie dough on a lightly floured surface to fit the top of the pie. You can create a lattice crust or a solid crust with vent holes. Trim any excess dough and crimp the edges to seal.
8. Brush the top crust with beaten egg and sprinkle with granulated sugar for a golden finish.
9. Place the pie on a baking sheet (to catch any drips) and bake in the preheated oven for 45-55 minutes, or until the crust is golden brown and the filling is bubbly.
10. Remove the pie from the oven and let it cool on a wire rack for at least 1 hour before slicing and serving.
11. Serve slices of Saskatoon berry pie warm or at room temperature, optionally with a scoop of vanilla ice cream or whipped cream on top.

Enjoy the delicious taste of Saskatchewan's prairie berries with this homemade Saskatoon berry pie!

Montreal bagels

Ingredients:

For the dough:

- 2 teaspoons active dry yeast
- 1 and 1/2 cups warm water
- 1/4 cup granulated sugar
- 4 cups bread flour
- 1 and 1/2 teaspoons salt

For boiling and topping:

- 1/4 cup honey or barley malt syrup
- 1 tablespoon granulated sugar
- 1 egg white, lightly beaten
- Optional toppings: sesame seeds, poppy seeds, or everything bagel seasoning

Instructions:

1. In a small bowl, combine the warm water, granulated sugar, and active dry yeast. Let it sit for about 5-10 minutes, or until foamy.
2. In a large mixing bowl or the bowl of a stand mixer fitted with a dough hook attachment, combine the bread flour and salt. Add the yeast mixture and mix until a rough dough forms.
3. Knead the dough for about 8-10 minutes, either by hand on a lightly floured surface or with a stand mixer, until it becomes smooth and elastic.
4. Shape the dough into a ball and place it in a lightly greased bowl. Cover with a clean kitchen towel or plastic wrap and let it rise in a warm, draft-free place for about 1-1.5 hours, or until doubled in size.
5. Once the dough has risen, punch it down and divide it into 12 equal-sized portions. Roll each portion into a rope about 10-12 inches long. Join the ends of each rope to form a bagel shape, pinching the ends together firmly.
6. Preheat your oven to 425°F (220°C). Line a baking sheet with parchment paper and lightly grease it.

7. In a large pot, bring water to a boil. Add the honey or barley malt syrup and granulated sugar to the boiling water and stir until dissolved.
8. Carefully lower the bagels, a few at a time, into the boiling water. Boil for about 30 seconds on each side, then remove them with a slotted spoon and place them on the prepared baking sheet.
9. Brush the tops of the boiled bagels with the beaten egg white and sprinkle with your choice of toppings, such as sesame seeds, poppy seeds, or everything bagel seasoning.
10. Bake the bagels in the preheated oven for 15-20 minutes, or until golden brown and cooked through.
11. Remove the bagels from the oven and let them cool on a wire rack before serving.

Enjoy these homemade Montreal bagels warm or toasted, with cream cheese, butter, or your favorite toppings!

Nova Scotia seafood chowder

Ingredients:

- 4 slices bacon, chopped
- 1 tablespoon unsalted butter
- 1 onion, diced
- 2 stalks celery, diced
- 2 cloves garlic, minced
- 2 tablespoons all-purpose flour
- 4 cups seafood or fish stock
- 1 cup whole milk
- 1 cup heavy cream
- 2 cups potatoes, peeled and diced
- 1 bay leaf
- 1/2 teaspoon dried thyme
- Salt and pepper, to taste
- 1 pound mixed seafood (e.g., lobster meat, scallops, shrimp, haddock), diced into bite-sized pieces
- 2 tablespoons fresh parsley, chopped (for garnish)

Instructions:

1. In a large pot or Dutch oven, cook the chopped bacon over medium heat until crisp. Remove the bacon with a slotted spoon and set aside, leaving the bacon fat in the pot.
2. Add the butter to the pot and melt it in the bacon fat. Add the diced onion and celery, and cook until softened, about 5 minutes. Add the minced garlic and cook for an additional minute.
3. Sprinkle the flour over the vegetables and cook, stirring constantly, for 2-3 minutes to make a roux.
4. Gradually pour in the seafood or fish stock, stirring constantly to prevent lumps from forming. Add the whole milk and heavy cream, stirring to combine.
5. Add the diced potatoes, bay leaf, dried thyme, salt, and pepper to the pot. Bring the mixture to a simmer and cook until the potatoes are tender, about 15-20 minutes.

6. Once the potatoes are tender, add the diced seafood to the pot and cook for an additional 5-7 minutes, or until the seafood is cooked through. Be careful not to overcook the seafood.
7. Taste the chowder and adjust the seasoning with salt and pepper, if needed. Remove the bay leaf from the pot.
8. Ladle the Nova Scotia seafood chowder into bowls and garnish with the reserved crispy bacon and chopped fresh parsley.
9. Serve the chowder hot, accompanied by crusty bread or oyster crackers for dipping.

Enjoy the rich and flavorful taste of Nova Scotia seafood chowder, perfect for warming up on chilly days or for a comforting meal any time of the year!

Montreal smoked meat sandwich

Ingredients:

- 1 lb Montreal smoked meat (available from delis or specialty shops)
- Rye bread slices
- Yellow or Dijon mustard
- Pickles, sliced (optional)
- Coleslaw (optional)

Instructions:

1. Start by thinly slicing the Montreal smoked meat. You can ask your butcher to slice it for you, or use a sharp knife to slice it at home.
2. Lightly toast the rye bread slices. This step is optional but can help to enhance the flavor and texture of the sandwich.
3. Spread a generous amount of mustard on one side of each slice of rye bread.
4. Pile the thinly sliced Montreal smoked meat onto one slice of the rye bread. Layer it as thick as you like, but traditionally Montreal smoked meat sandwiches are generously filled.
5. If desired, add a layer of sliced pickles on top of the smoked meat for a tangy crunch.
6. Optionally, add a scoop of coleslaw on top of the pickles for a refreshing contrast to the rich smoked meat.
7. Top the sandwich with the remaining slice of rye bread, mustard side down, to form a sandwich.
8. Slice the sandwich in half diagonally, if desired, and serve immediately.
9. Enjoy your homemade Montreal smoked meat sandwich with a side of additional pickles or your favorite accompaniments.

This classic Montreal delicacy is sure to satisfy your cravings for a flavorful and hearty sandwich experience!

Alberta beef steak

Ingredients:

- 2 Alberta beef steaks (such as ribeye, strip loin, or tenderloin), about 1 inch thick
- Salt and freshly ground black pepper
- Olive oil or vegetable oil, for cooking
- Optional: Steak seasoning or marinade of your choice

Instructions:

1. Remove the beef steaks from the refrigerator and let them come to room temperature for about 30 minutes before cooking. This helps ensure even cooking.
2. Preheat your grill, stovetop grill pan, or cast iron skillet over medium-high heat. You want the cooking surface to be hot to ensure a good sear on the steaks.
3. While the grill or skillet is heating up, season the beef steaks generously on both sides with salt and freshly ground black pepper. You can also use your favorite steak seasoning or marinade for additional flavor.
4. If using a grill, lightly brush the grill grates with oil to prevent sticking. If using a skillet, add a small amount of oil to the skillet and swirl to coat the bottom.
5. Carefully place the seasoned beef steaks on the hot grill or skillet. Cook the steaks for about 4-5 minutes on each side for medium-rare doneness, or adjust the cooking time according to your preferred level of doneness (see below for approximate cooking times).
6. Avoid flipping the steaks too frequently; allow them to develop a nice sear on each side before flipping.
7. Use an instant-read meat thermometer to check the internal temperature of the steaks. The following are approximate temperatures for different levels of doneness:
    - Rare: 120-125°F (49-52°C)
    - Medium rare: 130-135°F (54-57°C)
    - Medium: 140-145°F (60-63°C)
    - Medium well: 150-155°F (66-68°C)
    - Well done: 160°F (71°C) and above
8. Once the steaks reach your desired level of doneness, remove them from the grill or skillet and transfer them to a cutting board. Allow the steaks to rest for a few minutes before slicing and serving.

9. Serve the Alberta beef steaks hot, accompanied by your favorite side dishes such as roasted vegetables, mashed potatoes, or a fresh salad.

Enjoy the rich flavor and tender texture of Alberta beef steak, a delicious and satisfying meal that highlights the quality beef produced in the region!

Pacific salmon with maple glaze

Ingredients:

- 4 Pacific salmon fillets, skin-on or skinless, about 6 ounces each
- Salt and pepper, to taste
- 1/4 cup maple syrup
- 2 tablespoons soy sauce
- 1 tablespoon Dijon mustard
- 2 cloves garlic, minced
- 1 tablespoon olive oil
- Optional: Chopped fresh parsley or green onions for garnish

Instructions:

1. Preheat your oven to 400°F (200°C). Line a baking sheet with parchment paper or lightly grease it with oil.
2. Season the salmon fillets with salt and pepper on both sides. Place them on the prepared baking sheet, skin-side down if using skin-on fillets.
3. In a small bowl, whisk together the maple syrup, soy sauce, Dijon mustard, and minced garlic until well combined.
4. Brush the maple glaze over the top and sides of the salmon fillets, reserving some of the glaze for basting later.
5. Drizzle the olive oil over the salmon fillets to help keep them moist during baking.
6. Place the baking sheet in the preheated oven and bake the salmon for about 12-15 minutes, or until the fish is cooked through and flakes easily with a fork. The cooking time may vary depending on the thickness of the salmon fillets.
7. About halfway through the cooking time, baste the salmon fillets with the reserved maple glaze using a pastry brush.
8. Once the salmon is cooked, remove it from the oven and let it rest for a few minutes before serving.
9. Garnish the Pacific salmon with chopped fresh parsley or green onions, if desired.
10. Serve the maple-glazed salmon hot, accompanied by your favorite side dishes such as roasted vegetables, rice, or salad.

Enjoy the delicious combination of tender Pacific salmon with the sweet and savory flavors of the maple glaze, perfect for a special dinner or anytime you want to impress with a flavorful seafood dish!

Newfoundland cod au gratin

Ingredients:

- 1 lb cod fillets, skinless and boneless
- Salt and pepper, to taste
- 2 tablespoons butter
- 2 tablespoons all-purpose flour
- 1 cup milk
- 1/2 cup grated cheddar cheese
- 1/4 cup grated Parmesan cheese
- 1/2 cup breadcrumbs
- 1 tablespoon chopped fresh parsley (optional, for garnish)

Instructions:

1. Preheat your oven to 375°F (190°C). Grease a baking dish with butter or cooking spray.
2. Season the cod fillets with salt and pepper on both sides, then place them in the prepared baking dish in a single layer.
3. In a small saucepan, melt the butter over medium heat. Add the flour and cook, stirring constantly, for 1-2 minutes to make a roux.
4. Gradually whisk in the milk, stirring constantly to prevent lumps from forming. Cook the sauce until it thickens, about 3-5 minutes.
5. Remove the saucepan from the heat and stir in the grated cheddar cheese until melted and smooth. Season the sauce with additional salt and pepper, if needed.
6. Pour the cheese sauce over the cod fillets in the baking dish, making sure to cover them evenly.
7. In a small bowl, combine the grated Parmesan cheese and breadcrumbs. Sprinkle this mixture over the top of the cod and cheese sauce.
8. Bake the Newfoundland Cod au Gratin in the preheated oven for 20-25 minutes, or until the fish is cooked through and the topping is golden and crispy.
9. Once cooked, remove the baking dish from the oven and let it cool for a few minutes before serving.
10. Garnish the Cod au Gratin with chopped fresh parsley, if desired, and serve hot.

Enjoy the comforting flavors of this Newfoundland classic, perfect for a cozy family dinner or special occasion!

Blueberry grunt

Ingredients:

For the blueberry filling:

- 4 cups fresh or frozen blueberries
- 1/2 cup granulated sugar
- 1 tablespoon lemon juice
- 1/2 teaspoon ground cinnamon
- 1/4 teaspoon ground nutmeg
- 1/2 cup water

For the dumplings:

- 1 and 1/2 cups all-purpose flour
- 2 teaspoons baking powder
- 1/2 teaspoon salt
- 1/4 cup granulated sugar
- 1/2 cup milk
- 2 tablespoons unsalted butter, melted

Instructions:

1. In a large saucepan, combine the blueberries, granulated sugar, lemon juice, ground cinnamon, ground nutmeg, and water. Bring the mixture to a simmer over medium heat.
2. Reduce the heat to low and let the blueberry mixture simmer gently for about 10-15 minutes, stirring occasionally, until the berries have softened and released their juices. The mixture should thicken slightly.
3. While the blueberries are simmering, prepare the dumplings. In a mixing bowl, whisk together the flour, baking powder, salt, and granulated sugar.
4. Add the milk and melted butter to the dry ingredients, and stir until just combined. Be careful not to overmix; the dough should be slightly sticky.
5. Once the blueberry mixture is ready, drop spoonfuls of the dumpling dough on top of the simmering blueberries, making sure they are evenly spaced.
6. Cover the saucepan with a tight-fitting lid and let the dumplings cook undisturbed for about 15-20 minutes, or until they are cooked through and fluffy. Do not lift the lid while the dumplings are cooking, as this will allow steam to escape.

7. Once the dumplings are cooked, remove the saucepan from the heat and let it sit, covered, for a few minutes to allow the flavors to meld.
8. Serve the blueberry grunt warm, spooning the blueberry mixture and dumplings into bowls. You can serve it as is or with a dollop of whipped cream or a scoop of vanilla ice cream for extra indulgence.

Enjoy the comforting and fruity flavors of this classic Canadian dessert, perfect for any occasion!

Montreal-style bagels with smoked salmon

Ingredients:

- Montreal-style bagels (store-bought or homemade)
- Smoked salmon slices
- Cream cheese
- Red onion, thinly sliced
- Capers
- Fresh dill, chopped
- Lemon wedges

Instructions:

1. Slice the Montreal-style bagels in half horizontally.
2. Spread a generous layer of cream cheese on each half of the bagels.
3. Place slices of smoked salmon on the bottom halves of the bagels, covering the cream cheese.
4. Top the smoked salmon with thinly sliced red onion and a few capers.
5. Sprinkle chopped fresh dill over the toppings.
6. Squeeze a wedge of lemon over the smoked salmon, if desired, for a burst of citrus flavor.
7. Place the top halves of the bagels over the toppings to form sandwiches.
8. Serve the Montreal-style bagels with smoked salmon immediately, either as a breakfast or brunch dish, or as a light lunch or snack.
9. Enjoy the delicious combination of flavors and textures in these Montreal-style bagels with smoked salmon, perfect for any occasion!

Feel free to customize this recipe by adding other toppings such as sliced cucumber, tomato, or avocado, or by incorporating your favorite herbs or spices into the cream cheese spread.

Butter chicken poutine

Ingredients:

For the butter chicken:

- 1 lb boneless, skinless chicken breasts or thighs, cut into bite-sized pieces
- 2 tablespoons butter or ghee
- 1 onion, finely chopped
- 3 cloves garlic, minced
- 1 tablespoon grated fresh ginger
- 1 teaspoon ground turmeric
- 1 teaspoon ground cumin
- 1 teaspoon ground coriander
- 1 teaspoon garam masala
- 1/2 teaspoon paprika
- 1/4 teaspoon cayenne pepper (adjust to taste)
- 1 cup tomato puree or crushed tomatoes
- 1/2 cup heavy cream or coconut milk
- Salt and pepper, to taste
- Chopped fresh cilantro, for garnish

For the poutine:

- French fries, cooked according to package instructions
- Cheese curds
- Gravy (you can use store-bought gravy or make your own using beef or chicken broth)

Instructions:

1. In a large skillet or saucepan, melt the butter or ghee over medium heat. Add the chopped onion and cook until softened, about 5 minutes.
2. Add the minced garlic and grated ginger to the skillet, and cook for another 1-2 minutes, until fragrant.
3. Add the diced chicken pieces to the skillet, and cook until browned on all sides, about 5-7 minutes.

4. Stir in the ground turmeric, cumin, coriander, garam masala, paprika, and cayenne pepper, and cook for another minute until the spices are toasted and fragrant.
5. Pour in the tomato puree or crushed tomatoes, and stir to combine. Bring the mixture to a simmer, then reduce the heat to low and let it cook for 10-15 minutes, stirring occasionally, until the sauce has thickened slightly.
6. Stir in the heavy cream or coconut milk, and simmer for another 5 minutes. Season the butter chicken sauce with salt and pepper to taste.
7. While the butter chicken is simmering, prepare the French fries according to package instructions, and warm the gravy in a separate saucepan.
8. To assemble the poutine, place a generous serving of cooked French fries on a plate or in a bowl. Top the fries with cheese curds, and ladle the hot gravy over the top.
9. Spoon the butter chicken sauce over the cheese curds and gravy.
10. Garnish the butter chicken poutine with chopped fresh cilantro, and serve immediately.

Enjoy the delicious fusion of flavors in this butter chicken poutine, a unique twist on the classic Canadian dish!

Quebecois meat pie (tourtière du Lac-Saint-Jean)

Ingredients:

For the pastry crust:

- 2 and 1/2 cups all-purpose flour
- 1 cup cold unsalted butter, cut into small cubes
- 1 teaspoon salt
- 6-8 tablespoons ice water

For the filling:

- 1 lb ground pork
- 1/2 lb ground beef
- 1 onion, finely chopped
- 2 cloves garlic, minced
- 1/2 teaspoon ground cinnamon
- 1/4 teaspoon ground cloves
- 1/4 teaspoon ground nutmeg
- 1/4 teaspoon ground allspice
- Salt and pepper, to taste
- 1/2 cup beef or chicken broth
- 1/2 cup breadcrumbs
- 1 egg, beaten (for egg wash)

Instructions:

1. To make the pastry crust, combine the flour and salt in a large mixing bowl. Add the cold cubed butter and use a pastry cutter or your fingertips to work the butter into the flour until the mixture resembles coarse crumbs.
2. Gradually add the ice water, 1 tablespoon at a time, mixing with a fork until the dough comes together. Be careful not to overwork the dough.
3. Divide the dough into two equal portions, shape each portion into a disk, wrap them in plastic wrap, and refrigerate for at least 30 minutes.
4. Preheat your oven to 400°F (200°C).

5. In a large skillet, cook the ground pork and ground beef over medium heat until browned, breaking up any large chunks with a spoon.
6. Add the chopped onion and minced garlic to the skillet, and cook until softened, about 5 minutes.
7. Stir in the ground cinnamon, cloves, nutmeg, allspice, salt, and pepper, and cook for another minute until fragrant.
8. Pour in the beef or chicken broth and bring the mixture to a simmer. Cook for 5-7 minutes, or until most of the liquid has evaporated.
9. Remove the skillet from the heat and stir in the breadcrumbs. Let the filling mixture cool slightly.
10. Roll out one portion of the chilled pastry dough on a lightly floured surface to fit the bottom of a 9-inch pie dish. Place the rolled-out dough in the pie dish.
11. Spoon the cooled filling mixture into the pastry-lined pie dish, spreading it out evenly.
12. Roll out the remaining portion of pastry dough and place it over the top of the filling. Trim any excess dough and crimp the edges to seal.
13. Brush the top crust with beaten egg wash.
14. Use a sharp knife to make a few small slits in the top crust to allow steam to escape during baking.
15. Place the tourtière in the preheated oven and bake for 40-45 minutes, or until the crust is golden brown and the filling is bubbling.
16. Remove the tourtière from the oven and let it cool for a few minutes before slicing and serving.
17. Serve the tourtière du Lac-Saint-Jean warm, accompanied by your favorite condiments such as ketchup, cranberry sauce, or pickles.

Enjoy this delicious and comforting Quebecois meat pie, perfect for holiday gatherings or any special occasion!

Haddock and chips

Ingredients:

For the pastry crust:

- 2 and 1/2 cups all-purpose flour
- 1 cup cold unsalted butter, cut into small cubes
- 1 teaspoon salt
- 6-8 tablespoons ice water

For the filling:

- 1 lb ground pork
- 1/2 lb ground beef
- 1 onion, finely chopped
- 2 cloves garlic, minced
- 1/2 teaspoon ground cinnamon
- 1/4 teaspoon ground cloves
- 1/4 teaspoon ground nutmeg
- 1/4 teaspoon ground allspice
- Salt and pepper, to taste
- 1/2 cup beef or chicken broth
- 1/2 cup breadcrumbs
- 1 egg, beaten (for egg wash)

Instructions:

1. To make the pastry crust, combine the flour and salt in a large mixing bowl. Add the cold cubed butter and use a pastry cutter or your fingertips to work the butter into the flour until the mixture resembles coarse crumbs.
2. Gradually add the ice water, 1 tablespoon at a time, mixing with a fork until the dough comes together. Be careful not to overwork the dough.
3. Divide the dough into two equal portions, shape each portion into a disk, wrap them in plastic wrap, and refrigerate for at least 30 minutes.
4. Preheat your oven to 400°F (200°C).

5. In a large skillet, cook the ground pork and ground beef over medium heat until browned, breaking up any large chunks with a spoon.
6. Add the chopped onion and minced garlic to the skillet, and cook until softened, about 5 minutes.
7. Stir in the ground cinnamon, cloves, nutmeg, allspice, salt, and pepper, and cook for another minute until fragrant.
8. Pour in the beef or chicken broth and bring the mixture to a simmer. Cook for 5-7 minutes, or until most of the liquid has evaporated.
9. Remove the skillet from the heat and stir in the breadcrumbs. Let the filling mixture cool slightly.
10. Roll out one portion of the chilled pastry dough on a lightly floured surface to fit the bottom of a 9-inch pie dish. Place the rolled-out dough in the pie dish.
11. Spoon the cooled filling mixture into the pastry-lined pie dish, spreading it out evenly.
12. Roll out the remaining portion of pastry dough and place it over the top of the filling. Trim any excess dough and crimp the edges to seal.
13. Brush the top crust with beaten egg wash.
14. Use a sharp knife to make a few small slits in the top crust to allow steam to escape during baking.
15. Place the tourtière in the preheated oven and bake for 40-45 minutes, or until the crust is golden brown and the filling is bubbling.
16. Remove the tourtière from the oven and let it cool for a few minutes before slicing and serving.
17. Serve the tourtière du Lac-Saint-Jean warm, accompanied by your favorite condiments such as ketchup, cranberry sauce, or pickles.

Enjoy this delicious and comforting Quebecois meat pie, perfect for holiday gatherings or any special occasion!

Timbits

Ingredients:

For the doughnuts:

- 2 and 1/4 cups all-purpose flour
- 1/4 cup granulated sugar
- 1 tablespoon baking powder
- 1/2 teaspoon salt
- 1/2 cup milk
- 1/4 cup unsalted butter, melted
- 1 large egg
- 1 teaspoon vanilla extract
- Vegetable oil, for frying

For the glaze:

- 2 cups powdered sugar
- 1/4 cup milk
- 1/2 teaspoon vanilla extract

Instructions:

1. In a large mixing bowl, whisk together the flour, sugar, baking powder, and salt.
2. In a separate bowl, whisk together the milk, melted butter, egg, and vanilla extract.
3. Pour the wet ingredients into the dry ingredients and stir until a soft dough forms. Be careful not to overmix.
4. Turn the dough out onto a lightly floured surface and knead gently a few times until smooth. Roll out the dough to about 1/2 inch thickness.
5. Use a small round cutter or teaspoon to cut out small doughnut holes from the dough. Place the doughnut holes on a baking sheet lined with parchment paper.
6. Heat vegetable oil in a deep fryer or heavy-bottomed pot to 350°F (175°C).
7. Carefully drop the doughnut holes into the hot oil, a few at a time, making sure not to overcrowd the pot. Fry for about 2-3 minutes, turning occasionally, until golden brown and cooked through.

8. Use a slotted spoon to transfer the fried doughnut holes to a wire rack set over a baking sheet to drain and cool.
9. To make the glaze, whisk together the powdered sugar, milk, and vanilla extract in a shallow bowl until smooth.
10. Dip each cooled doughnut hole into the glaze, coating it completely, then return it to the wire rack to allow any excess glaze to drip off.
11. Allow the glaze to set for a few minutes before serving.
12. Enjoy your homemade Timbits as a delicious snack or dessert!

Feel free to customize your Timbits by adding different flavors or toppings to the glaze, such as cocoa powder, sprinkles, or crushed nuts.

Saskatoon berry muffins

Ingredients:

- 2 cups all-purpose flour
- 1/2 cup granulated sugar
- 2 teaspoons baking powder
- 1/2 teaspoon baking soda
- 1/2 teaspoon salt
- 1/2 cup unsalted butter, melted and cooled
- 2 large eggs
- 1 cup plain Greek yogurt (or sour cream)
- 1 teaspoon vanilla extract
- 1 and 1/2 cups fresh or frozen Saskatoon berries (if using frozen, do not thaw)

Instructions:

1. Preheat your oven to 375°F (190°C). Line a muffin tin with paper liners or grease the muffin cups with butter or cooking spray.
2. In a large mixing bowl, whisk together the flour, sugar, baking powder, baking soda, and salt until well combined.
3. In another bowl, whisk together the melted butter, eggs, Greek yogurt, and vanilla extract until smooth.
4. Pour the wet ingredients into the dry ingredients and stir until just combined. Do not overmix; the batter should be lumpy.
5. Gently fold in the Saskatoon berries until evenly distributed throughout the batter.
6. Spoon the batter into the prepared muffin cups, filling each about 2/3 full.
7. Optional: Sprinkle a little granulated sugar on top of each muffin for a sweet crunch.
8. Bake the muffins in the preheated oven for 18-22 minutes, or until the tops are golden brown and a toothpick inserted into the center comes out clean.
9. Remove the muffins from the oven and let them cool in the muffin tin for a few minutes before transferring them to a wire rack to cool completely.
10. Enjoy your homemade Saskatoon berry muffins warm or at room temperature. They're perfect for breakfast, brunch, or as a snack any time of day!

Feel free to adjust the amount of sugar according to your taste preference, and you can also add a streusel topping for extra texture and flavor. Enjoy these delicious muffins bursting with the flavor of Saskatoon berries!

Maple-glazed donuts

Ingredients:

For the donuts:

- 2 and 1/4 cups all-purpose flour
- 1 and 1/2 teaspoons baking powder
- 1/2 teaspoon baking soda
- 1/2 teaspoon salt
- 1/2 teaspoon ground nutmeg
- 1/2 cup granulated sugar
- 2 tablespoons unsalted butter, melted
- 1/2 cup buttermilk
- 2 large eggs
- 1 teaspoon vanilla extract

For the maple glaze:

- 1 cup powdered sugar
- 2 tablespoons pure maple syrup
- 1-2 tablespoons milk
- 1/2 teaspoon vanilla extract

Instructions:

1. Preheat your oven to 350°F (175°C). Grease a donut pan with non-stick cooking spray.
2. In a large mixing bowl, whisk together the flour, baking powder, baking soda, salt, nutmeg, and granulated sugar until well combined.
3. In a separate bowl, whisk together the melted butter, buttermilk, eggs, and vanilla extract until smooth.
4. Pour the wet ingredients into the dry ingredients and stir until just combined. Do not overmix; the batter should be slightly lumpy.
5. Spoon the batter into the prepared donut pan, filling each cavity about 2/3 full.
6. Bake the donuts in the preheated oven for 10-12 minutes, or until lightly golden and a toothpick inserted into the center comes out clean.

7. Remove the donuts from the oven and let them cool in the pan for a few minutes before transferring them to a wire rack to cool completely.
8. While the donuts are cooling, make the maple glaze. In a small bowl, whisk together the powdered sugar, maple syrup, milk, and vanilla extract until smooth. Add more milk as needed to achieve your desired consistency.
9. Once the donuts are completely cooled, dip each donut into the maple glaze, allowing any excess glaze to drip off.
10. Place the glazed donuts back on the wire rack to allow the glaze to set for a few minutes.
11. Enjoy your homemade maple-glazed donuts with a cup of coffee or your favorite hot beverage!

Feel free to customize these donuts by adding chopped nuts, sprinkles, or even crispy bacon bits on top of the glaze for extra flavor and texture.

Elk burgers

Ingredients:

- 1 lb ground elk meat
- 1/4 cup breadcrumbs
- 1/4 cup grated onion
- 1 clove garlic, minced
- 1 teaspoon Worcestershire sauce
- 1/2 teaspoon salt
- 1/4 teaspoon black pepper
- Burger buns
- Optional toppings: lettuce, tomato, onion, cheese, pickles, condiments

Instructions:

1. In a large mixing bowl, combine the ground elk meat, breadcrumbs, grated onion, minced garlic, Worcestershire sauce, salt, and pepper. Use your hands to gently mix everything together until well combined.
2. Divide the mixture into 4 equal portions and shape each portion into a patty, about 1/2 to 3/4 inch thick. Make a slight indentation in the center of each patty with your thumb to prevent it from puffing up while cooking.
3. Preheat your grill or grill pan to medium-high heat. If using a grill pan, lightly oil the surface to prevent sticking.
4. Place the elk burger patties on the grill or grill pan and cook for about 4-5 minutes per side, or until they reach your desired level of doneness. Avoid pressing down on the patties with a spatula while cooking, as this can cause them to lose moisture.
5. If adding cheese, place a slice of cheese on top of each burger during the last minute of cooking and allow it to melt.
6. While the burgers are cooking, toast the burger buns on the grill until lightly golden and warmed through.
7. Once the elk burgers are cooked to your liking, remove them from the grill and let them rest for a few minutes.
8. Assemble the burgers by placing each patty on a toasted bun and adding your desired toppings, such as lettuce, tomato, onion, pickles, or condiments.
9. Serve the elk burgers immediately with your favorite sides, such as fries, coleslaw, or a salad.

Enjoy your delicious homemade elk burgers, featuring lean and flavorful elk meat!

Wild rice pilaf

Ingredients:

- 1 cup wild rice
- 2 cups chicken or vegetable broth
- 1 tablespoon olive oil or butter
- 1 small onion, finely chopped
- 2 cloves garlic, minced
- 1 carrot, diced
- 1 celery stalk, diced
- 1/4 cup chopped mushrooms (optional)
- 1/4 cup chopped almonds or pecans (optional)
- Salt and pepper, to taste
- Fresh parsley, chopped (for garnish)

Instructions:

1. Rinse the wild rice under cold water in a fine-mesh sieve to remove any debris.
2. In a medium saucepan, bring the chicken or vegetable broth to a boil. Add the rinsed wild rice, reduce the heat to low, cover, and simmer for about 45-50 minutes, or until the rice is tender and most of the liquid is absorbed. Drain any excess liquid if necessary.
3. In a large skillet, heat the olive oil or butter over medium heat. Add the chopped onion and cook until softened, about 3-4 minutes.
4. Add the minced garlic to the skillet and cook for another 1-2 minutes, until fragrant.
5. Stir in the diced carrot, diced celery, chopped mushrooms (if using), and chopped almonds or pecans (if using). Cook for 5-6 minutes, or until the vegetables are tender.
6. Add the cooked wild rice to the skillet with the sautéed vegetables and nuts. Stir to combine.
7. Season the wild rice pilaf with salt and pepper to taste. You can also add additional herbs and spices if desired, such as dried thyme, rosemary, or sage.
8. Cook the wild rice pilaf for a few more minutes, stirring occasionally, until heated through.
9. Remove the skillet from the heat and transfer the wild rice pilaf to a serving dish.
10. Garnish with freshly chopped parsley before serving.

Enjoy your homemade wild rice pilaf as a flavorful and nutritious side dish alongside your favorite main courses!

Atlantic lobster bisque

Ingredients:

- 2 live Atlantic lobsters (about 1 1/2 to 2 pounds each)
- 4 tablespoons unsalted butter
- 1 onion, chopped
- 2 carrots, chopped
- 2 celery stalks, chopped
- 2 garlic cloves, minced
- 1/4 cup tomato paste
- 1/4 cup all-purpose flour
- 4 cups seafood or chicken broth
- 1 cup dry white wine
- 1 cup heavy cream
- 2 bay leaves
- 1/2 teaspoon dried thyme
- Salt and pepper, to taste
- Chopped fresh parsley, for garnish

Instructions:

1. Fill a large pot with water and bring it to a boil. Add the live lobsters and cook for about 8-10 minutes, or until they turn bright red and are cooked through. Remove the lobsters from the pot and let them cool slightly.
2. Once the lobsters are cool enough to handle, remove the meat from the shells. Reserve the shells for making lobster stock.
3. Chop the lobster meat into bite-sized pieces and set aside.
4. In a large soup pot or Dutch oven, melt the butter over medium heat. Add the chopped onion, carrots, and celery, and cook for about 5 minutes, or until the vegetables are softened.
5. Add the minced garlic and tomato paste to the pot, and cook for another 2-3 minutes, stirring constantly.
6. Sprinkle the flour over the vegetables and cook for 1-2 minutes, stirring constantly, to make a roux.
7. Gradually pour in the seafood or chicken broth and white wine, stirring constantly to prevent lumps from forming.

8. Add the bay leaves, dried thyme, salt, and pepper to the pot. Bring the mixture to a simmer and cook for about 15-20 minutes, or until the vegetables are tender and the flavors have melded together.
9. Remove the bay leaves from the pot and discard.
10. Use an immersion blender to puree the soup until smooth. Alternatively, you can transfer the soup in batches to a blender and puree until smooth, then return it to the pot.
11. Stir in the heavy cream and chopped lobster meat, and cook for another 5-10 minutes, or until the lobster is heated through and the soup is creamy and thickened.
12. Taste the bisque and adjust the seasoning with salt and pepper, if necessary.
13. Ladle the Atlantic lobster bisque into serving bowls and garnish with chopped fresh parsley.
14. Serve the bisque hot, accompanied by crusty bread or oyster crackers.

Enjoy the rich and luxurious flavors of this Atlantic lobster bisque, perfect for a special occasion or a cozy dinner at home!

PEI potato scallops

Ingredients:

- 4-5 medium-sized potatoes, peeled and thinly sliced
- 1 onion, thinly sliced
- 1/4 cup butter, melted
- 1/4 cup all-purpose flour
- 2 cups milk
- Salt and pepper, to taste
- 1 cup shredded cheddar cheese (optional)
- Chopped fresh parsley, for garnish (optional)

Instructions:

1. Preheat your oven to 375°F (190°C). Grease a baking dish with butter or cooking spray.
2. In a saucepan, melt the butter over medium heat. Add the flour and cook, stirring constantly, for 1-2 minutes to make a roux.
3. Gradually whisk in the milk, stirring constantly to prevent lumps from forming. Cook the sauce until thickened, about 5 minutes.
4. Season the sauce with salt and pepper to taste.
5. Arrange a layer of thinly sliced potatoes in the bottom of the greased baking dish, followed by a layer of sliced onions. Repeat the layers until all the potatoes and onions are used up, ending with a layer of potatoes on top.
6. Pour the thickened sauce over the layered potatoes and onions, making sure to evenly coat them.
7. If desired, sprinkle shredded cheddar cheese over the top of the potatoes.
8. Cover the baking dish with aluminum foil and bake in the preheated oven for 45-50 minutes, or until the potatoes are tender when pierced with a fork.
9. Remove the foil and continue baking for an additional 10-15 minutes, or until the top is golden brown and bubbly.
10. Once the PEI potato scallops are done baking, remove them from the oven and let them cool for a few minutes.
11. Garnish with chopped fresh parsley, if desired, before serving.
12. Serve the PEI potato scallops hot as a delicious side dish alongside roasted meats, poultry, or fish.

Enjoy the comforting flavors of these PEI potato scallops, a classic dish that celebrates the delicious taste of Prince Edward Island potatoes!

Nova Scotia blueberry grunt

Ingredients:

For the blueberry filling:

- 4 cups fresh or frozen blueberries
- 1/2 cup granulated sugar
- 1 tablespoon lemon juice
- 1/2 teaspoon ground cinnamon
- 1/4 teaspoon ground nutmeg
- 1/4 cup water

For the dumplings:

- 1 cup all-purpose flour
- 2 tablespoons granulated sugar
- 1 and 1/2 teaspoons baking powder
- 1/2 teaspoon salt
- 3 tablespoons cold unsalted butter, cut into small pieces
- 1/2 cup milk

Instructions:

1. In a large saucepan, combine the blueberries, sugar, lemon juice, cinnamon, nutmeg, and water. Stir well to combine.
2. Bring the blueberry mixture to a simmer over medium heat. Cook, stirring occasionally, for about 5-7 minutes, or until the blueberries start to release their juices and the mixture thickens slightly.
3. While the blueberry mixture is cooking, prepare the dumplings. In a mixing bowl, whisk together the flour, sugar, baking powder, and salt.
4. Cut the cold butter into the flour mixture using a pastry cutter or your fingers, until the mixture resembles coarse crumbs.
5. Gradually add the milk to the flour mixture, stirring until a soft dough forms. Be careful not to overmix.
6. Once the blueberry mixture has thickened, drop spoonfuls of the dumpling dough onto the surface of the blueberries, spacing them evenly.

7. Cover the saucepan with a tight-fitting lid and reduce the heat to low. Allow the dumplings to steam for about 15-20 minutes, or until they are cooked through and fluffy.
8. Once the dumplings are cooked, remove the saucepan from the heat and let it sit, covered, for a few minutes to allow the flavors to meld.
9. Serve the Nova Scotia blueberry grunt warm, spooning the blueberry mixture and dumplings into serving bowls.
10. Enjoy your delicious homemade blueberry grunt as is or with a dollop of whipped cream or a scoop of vanilla ice cream on top.

This Nova Scotia blueberry grunt is a comforting and satisfying dessert that celebrates the abundance of fresh blueberries in the region. Enjoy its rustic charm and delightful flavors!

Butter tart squares

Ingredients:

For the crust:

- 1 and 1/2 cups all-purpose flour
- 1/2 cup unsalted butter, cold and cubed
- 1/4 cup granulated sugar
- Pinch of salt

For the filling:

- 1/2 cup unsalted butter, melted
- 1 cup packed brown sugar
- 2 large eggs
- 1 teaspoon vanilla extract
- 1/4 cup all-purpose flour
- 1/2 teaspoon baking powder
- 1/4 teaspoon salt
- 1 cup raisins or chopped pecans (optional)

Instructions:

1. Preheat your oven to 350°F (175°C). Grease or line a 9x9-inch baking pan with parchment paper, leaving some overhang for easy removal.
2. In a mixing bowl, combine the flour, sugar, and salt for the crust. Cut in the cold cubed butter using a pastry cutter or fork until the mixture resembles coarse crumbs.
3. Press the crust mixture evenly into the bottom of the prepared baking pan. Bake in the preheated oven for 15-18 minutes, or until lightly golden. Remove from the oven and set aside.
4. In another mixing bowl, whisk together the melted butter, brown sugar, eggs, and vanilla extract until smooth.
5. Add the flour, baking powder, and salt to the wet ingredients, and stir until well combined.
6. If using, stir in the raisins or chopped pecans until evenly distributed.

7. Pour the filling over the baked crust and spread it out evenly.
8. Return the pan to the oven and bake for an additional 20-25 minutes, or until the filling is set and golden brown on top.
9. Remove the butter tart squares from the oven and let them cool completely in the pan on a wire rack.
10. Once cooled, use the parchment paper overhang to lift the squares out of the pan. Place them on a cutting board and cut into squares or bars.
11. Serve the butter tart squares at room temperature and enjoy!

These butter tart squares are sweet, gooey, and utterly delicious, making them a beloved Canadian treat for dessert or a sweet snack. Feel free to customize them by adding your favorite nuts or dried fruits to the filling.

Pemmican

Ingredients:

- 1 lb lean meat (such as beef, bison, venison, or elk)
- 1/2 lb rendered fat (such as beef tallow or lard)
- Optional: dried fruit (such as berries or raisins)

Instructions:

1. Start by drying the meat. You can do this by slicing it thinly and placing it on a wire rack in a low-temperature oven (around 150°F or 65°C) for several hours, or until it is completely dried and leathery. Alternatively, you can use a food dehydrator to dry the meat.
2. Once the meat is dried, grind it into a fine powder using a food processor or mortar and pestle. This will help make the pemmican easier to chew and digest.
3. If using dried fruit, chop it into small pieces.
4. In a large bowl, combine the dried meat powder and dried fruit (if using).
5. In a separate saucepan, melt the rendered fat over low heat until it is completely liquid.
6. Pour the melted fat over the meat mixture and stir until everything is well combined.
7. Line a shallow baking dish or tray with parchment paper.
8. Pour the pemmican mixture into the lined dish and spread it out evenly.
9. Place the dish in the refrigerator to chill until the pemmican is firm and set.
10. Once chilled, cut the pemmican into squares or bars for easy portioning.
11. Store the pemmican in an airtight container or wrap it tightly in wax paper. It can be kept at room temperature for several months or refrigerated for even longer storage.

Pemmican is a versatile food that can be eaten on its own as a high-energy snack or used as a component in other dishes. It's a nutritious and convenient option for anyone looking for a portable and long-lasting source of sustenance.

Quebecois pea soup (soupe aux pois)

Ingredients:

- 2 cups dried yellow split peas
- 8 cups water or vegetable broth
- 1 onion, chopped
- 2 carrots, chopped
- 2 celery stalks, chopped
- 2 cloves garlic, minced
- 1 bay leaf
- 1 teaspoon dried thyme
- 1/2 teaspoon dried marjoram
- 1/2 teaspoon dried savory
- 1 smoked ham hock or ham bone (optional, for flavor)
- Salt and pepper, to taste
- 1 tablespoon olive oil or butter
- 2 tablespoons maple syrup (optional, for sweetness)
- Chopped fresh parsley, for garnish (optional)

Instructions:

1. Rinse the dried split peas under cold water and pick out any debris or stones.
2. In a large soup pot or Dutch oven, heat the olive oil or butter over medium heat. Add the chopped onion, carrots, and celery, and cook until softened, about 5-7 minutes.
3. Add the minced garlic to the pot and cook for another 1-2 minutes, until fragrant.
4. Stir in the dried split peas, bay leaf, dried thyme, dried marjoram, and dried savory.
5. Pour in the water or vegetable broth and add the smoked ham hock or ham bone (if using) for extra flavor.
6. Bring the soup to a boil, then reduce the heat to low and simmer, partially covered, for about 1 to 1 1/2 hours, or until the split peas are soft and the soup has thickened. Stir occasionally to prevent sticking.
7. Once the soup is cooked and the split peas are tender, remove the ham hock or ham bone from the pot and discard.
8. If desired, use an immersion blender to partially blend the soup until it reaches your desired consistency. Alternatively, you can leave the soup as is for a chunkier texture.

9. Season the soup with salt and pepper to taste. If using maple syrup, stir it into the soup for a touch of sweetness.
10. Ladle the Quebecois pea soup into bowls and garnish with chopped fresh parsley, if desired.
11. Serve the soup hot with crusty bread or rolls on the side.

Enjoy this delicious and comforting Quebecois pea soup, packed with hearty flavor and wholesome ingredients!

Montreal-style steak seasoning

Ingredients:

- 2 tablespoons paprika
- 2 tablespoons black pepper
- 2 tablespoons kosher salt
- 1 tablespoon garlic powder
- 1 tablespoon onion powder
- 1 tablespoon dried coriander
- 1 tablespoon dried dill
- 1 tablespoon dried parsley
- 1 teaspoon red pepper flakes (optional, for heat)

Instructions:

1. In a small bowl, combine all the ingredients: paprika, black pepper, kosher salt, garlic powder, onion powder, dried coriander, dried dill, dried parsley, and red pepper flakes (if using).
2. Stir the spices together until well combined.
3. Transfer the Montreal-style steak seasoning to an airtight container or spice jar for storage.
4. To use the seasoning, generously sprinkle it over both sides of your steak (or other meat) before grilling, pan-searing, or roasting. Press the seasoning into the meat to help it adhere.
5. Cook the meat according to your preferred method until it reaches your desired level of doneness.
6. Let the meat rest for a few minutes before serving to allow the flavors to meld.
7. Enjoy your deliciously seasoned Montreal-style steak!

This homemade Montreal-style steak seasoning is sure to add fantastic flavor to your favorite cuts of meat, giving them that classic Montreal steakhouse taste. Adjust the amount of red pepper flakes to control the level of heat according to your preference.

Maritime seafood boil

Ingredients:

- 4-6 live lobsters
- 1 lb crab legs
- 1 lb large shrimp, deveined and shell-on
- 2 lbs mussels, cleaned and debearded
- 2 lbs littleneck clams, cleaned
- 1 lb baby potatoes, washed
- 4 ears of corn, husked and halved
- 1 lemon, cut into wedges
- Old Bay seasoning or seafood boil seasoning mix
- Salt, to taste
- Butter, melted (for serving)
- Cocktail sauce (for serving)
- Lemon wedges (for serving)

Instructions:

1. Fill a large stockpot or outdoor boiler with water, leaving enough space to accommodate all the seafood and other ingredients.
2. Bring the water to a rolling boil over high heat. Season the boiling water generously with Old Bay seasoning or seafood boil seasoning mix, as well as a pinch of salt.
3. Once the water is boiling and seasoned, add the baby potatoes and cook for about 10-15 minutes, or until they are just tender when pierced with a fork.
4. Add the halved ears of corn to the pot and continue to boil for another 5 minutes.
5. Carefully add the live lobsters to the pot, head first, and cover with a lid. Cook the lobsters for about 10-12 minutes, or until they turn bright red and are cooked through.
6. Add the crab legs to the pot and cook for an additional 5 minutes.
7. Finally, add the shrimp, mussels, and littleneck clams to the pot, making sure they are submerged in the boiling water. Cover with the lid and cook for about 5-7 minutes, or until the shrimp are pink and opaque, and the mussels and clams have opened.

8. Once all the seafood is cooked, carefully remove everything from the pot using a slotted spoon or a spider strainer, and transfer to a large serving platter or a newspaper-lined table.
9. Serve the Maritime seafood boil hot, with melted butter, cocktail sauce, and lemon wedges on the side for dipping.
10. Enjoy the feast with friends and family, using your hands and plenty of napkins to savor every delicious bite!

Feel free to customize your Maritime seafood boil by adding other seafood or vegetables of your choice, and adjust the seasoning according to your taste preferences. This communal dining experience is not only delicious but also a fun and festive way to celebrate the bounty of the sea.

Canadian bacon and pineapple pizza

Ingredients:

- 1 pre-made pizza dough (homemade or store-bought)
- 1/2 cup pizza sauce
- 1 cup shredded mozzarella cheese
- 1 cup diced Canadian bacon (or ham)
- 1 cup pineapple chunks (fresh or canned)
- Red pepper flakes (optional, for heat)
- Fresh basil leaves, torn (optional, for garnish)

Instructions:

1. Preheat your oven to the temperature recommended for your pizza dough (usually around 450°F or 230°C). If using a pizza stone, place it in the oven to preheat as well.
2. Roll out the pizza dough on a lightly floured surface to your desired thickness. Transfer the dough to a pizza peel or parchment paper-lined baking sheet.
3. Spread the pizza sauce evenly over the dough, leaving a small border around the edges for the crust.
4. Sprinkle the shredded mozzarella cheese over the sauce, covering the entire surface of the pizza.
5. Scatter the diced Canadian bacon (or ham) and pineapple chunks evenly over the cheese.
6. If desired, sprinkle red pepper flakes over the toppings for a touch of heat.
7. Carefully transfer the pizza to the preheated oven, either directly onto the pizza stone or onto the baking sheet.
8. Bake the pizza for about 12-15 minutes, or until the crust is golden brown and the cheese is bubbly and melted.
9. Once the pizza is done baking, remove it from the oven and let it cool for a few minutes.
10. If desired, garnish the pizza with torn fresh basil leaves for added flavor and freshness.
11. Slice the Canadian bacon and pineapple pizza into wedges and serve hot.

Enjoy this classic Canadian bacon and pineapple pizza as a delicious and satisfying meal, perfect for pizza nights or any casual gathering with friends and family! Feel free to customize the toppings to suit your taste preferences.

Alberta beef chili

Ingredients:

- 1 lb ground beef (preferably Alberta beef)
- 1 onion, diced
- 3 cloves garlic, minced
- 1 bell pepper, diced
- 1 can (14 oz) diced tomatoes
- 1 can (14 oz) kidney beans, drained and rinsed
- 1 can (14 oz) black beans, drained and rinsed
- 1 cup beef broth
- 2 tablespoons tomato paste
- 1 tablespoon chili powder
- 1 teaspoon ground cumin
- 1 teaspoon smoked paprika
- 1/2 teaspoon dried oregano
- Salt and pepper, to taste
- Optional toppings: shredded cheese, sour cream, chopped cilantro, sliced green onions

Instructions:

1. In a large pot or Dutch oven, cook the ground beef over medium heat until browned and cooked through, breaking it up with a spoon as it cooks.
2. Add the diced onion, minced garlic, and diced bell pepper to the pot with the cooked beef. Cook for another 3-4 minutes, or until the vegetables are softened.
3. Stir in the diced tomatoes (with their juices), drained and rinsed kidney beans, drained and rinsed black beans, beef broth, tomato paste, chili powder, ground cumin, smoked paprika, dried oregano, salt, and pepper.
4. Bring the chili to a simmer, then reduce the heat to low. Cover the pot and let the chili simmer for about 30-40 minutes, stirring occasionally, to allow the flavors to meld and the chili to thicken.
5. Taste the chili and adjust the seasoning with salt and pepper, if needed.
6. Once the chili is done cooking, remove it from the heat and let it sit for a few minutes before serving.
7. Serve the Alberta beef chili hot, garnished with your favorite toppings such as shredded cheese, sour cream, chopped cilantro, and sliced green onions.

8. Enjoy the hearty and flavorful Alberta beef chili with crusty bread, cornbread, or tortilla chips on the side.

This Alberta beef chili is sure to be a hit with family and friends, and it's perfect for cozy dinners or game day gatherings. Feel free to customize the chili with additional vegetables, spices, or toppings to suit your taste preferences.

Maple syrup bacon-wrapped scallops

Ingredients:

- 12 large sea scallops, thawed if frozen
- 6 slices of bacon, cut in half crosswise
- 1/4 cup maple syrup
- 1 tablespoon olive oil
- Salt and pepper, to taste
- Toothpicks or skewers

Instructions:

1. Preheat your oven to 400°F (200°C). Line a baking sheet with parchment paper or aluminum foil for easy cleanup.
2. Rinse the scallops under cold water and pat them dry with paper towels. Season them lightly with salt and pepper.
3. Cut each slice of bacon in half crosswise, creating two shorter strips from each slice.
4. Wrap each scallop with a half-strip of bacon, securing it with a toothpick or skewer to hold it in place. Repeat with the remaining scallops and bacon.
5. In a small bowl, mix together the maple syrup and olive oil. Brush the mixture over each bacon-wrapped scallop, coating them evenly on all sides.
6. Place the bacon-wrapped scallops on the prepared baking sheet, leaving some space between each one to ensure even cooking.
7. Bake the scallops in the preheated oven for 15-20 minutes, or until the bacon is crispy and the scallops are cooked through. You can also broil them for the last few minutes to crisp up the bacon further, if desired.
8. Once cooked, remove the maple syrup bacon-wrapped scallops from the oven and let them cool for a few minutes before serving.
9. Transfer the scallops to a serving platter and remove the toothpicks or skewers before serving.
10. Garnish the maple syrup bacon-wrapped scallops with chopped fresh parsley or chives, if desired, and serve them hot as a delicious appetizer.

Enjoy these irresistible maple syrup bacon-wrapped scallops at your next gathering or special occasion! They're sure to be a crowd-pleaser with their perfect balance of sweet, savory, and salty flavors.

Haskap berry jam

Ingredients:

- 4 cups haskap berries, washed and stemmed
- 2 cups granulated sugar
- 1 tablespoon lemon juice
- 1 tablespoon pectin (optional, for thickening)

Instructions:

1. In a large saucepan, combine the haskap berries and granulated sugar. Stir to coat the berries evenly with the sugar.
2. Let the berries sit at room temperature for about 30 minutes to allow them to release their juices.
3. After 30 minutes, place the saucepan over medium heat and bring the berry mixture to a gentle boil, stirring occasionally.
4. Once the mixture reaches a boil, reduce the heat to low and let it simmer for about 15-20 minutes, or until the berries are soft and the mixture has thickened slightly.
5. Stir in the lemon juice and pectin (if using), and continue to cook for an additional 5 minutes.
6. Remove the saucepan from the heat and let the jam cool slightly.
7. Transfer the jam to sterilized jars, leaving about 1/4 inch of space at the top of each jar.
8. Seal the jars with lids and rings, and process them in a boiling water bath for 10 minutes to ensure proper sealing, or store the jam in the refrigerator for immediate use.
9. Once cooled, the haskap berry jam is ready to enjoy! Spread it on toast, muffins, scones, or use it as a topping for yogurt or ice cream.
10. Store any leftover jam in the refrigerator for up to several weeks.

Enjoy the delicious flavor of homemade haskap berry jam, bursting with the unique taste of these delightful berries!

Newfoundland toutons with molasses

Ingredients:

For the toutons:

- 2 cups all-purpose flour
- 1 teaspoon sugar
- 1/2 teaspoon salt
- 1 teaspoon baking powder
- 1 cup milk
- Vegetable oil, for frying

For serving:

- Molasses or syrup
- Butter (optional)

Instructions:

1. In a large mixing bowl, whisk together the flour, sugar, salt, and baking powder.
2. Gradually add the milk to the dry ingredients, stirring until a smooth batter forms. The batter should be thick but pourable. If it's too thick, you can add a little more milk.
3. Heat a skillet or frying pan over medium heat and add enough vegetable oil to coat the bottom of the pan.
4. Once the oil is hot, spoon about 1/4 cup of batter into the skillet for each touton, spreading it out slightly to form a round shape. You can cook multiple toutons at a time, depending on the size of your skillet.
5. Cook the toutons for 2-3 minutes on each side, or until they are golden brown and cooked through. Use a spatula to flip them halfway through cooking.
6. Once cooked, transfer the toutons to a paper towel-lined plate to drain off any excess oil.
7. Serve the toutons hot with a generous drizzle of molasses or syrup. You can also spread them with butter if desired.
8. Enjoy your delicious Newfoundland toutons with molasses for breakfast, brunch, or as a tasty snack!

These traditional Newfoundland toutons with molasses are sure to be a hit with their irresistible combination of crispy fried dough and sweet molasses flavor. They're a comforting and satisfying treat that's perfect for enjoying with family and friends.

Arctic char with dill sauce

Ingredients:

- 4 Arctic char fillets
- Salt and pepper, to taste
- 2 tablespoons olive oil
- 2 tablespoons butter
- 2 garlic cloves, minced
- 1/4 cup dry white wine
- 1 cup heavy cream
- 2 tablespoons fresh dill, chopped
- Lemon wedges, for serving

Instructions:

1. Prepare the Arctic Char:
    - Season the Arctic char fillets with salt and pepper on both sides.
    - Heat olive oil in a large skillet over medium-high heat.
    - Place the fillets skin-side down in the skillet and cook for about 4-5 minutes until the skin is crispy and golden. Flip and cook for another 3-4 minutes until the fish is cooked through. Remove from skillet and set aside.
2. Make the Dill Sauce:
    - In the same skillet, melt the butter over medium heat.
    - Add minced garlic and sauté for about 1 minute until fragrant.
    - Pour in the white wine and let it simmer for 2-3 minutes until slightly reduced.
    - Stir in the heavy cream and chopped dill. Let the sauce simmer for another 2-3 minutes until it thickens slightly.
    - Season the sauce with salt and pepper to taste.
3. Serve:
    - Place the cooked Arctic char fillets on serving plates.
    - Spoon the dill sauce over the fillets.
    - Garnish with additional fresh dill if desired and serve with lemon wedges on the side.

This dish pairs wonderfully with steamed vegetables, roasted potatoes, or a simple green salad. Enjoy your Arctic char with dill sauce!

Butter tart ice cream

Ingredients:

- 2 cups heavy cream
- 1 cup whole milk
- 3/4 cup brown sugar
- 4 large egg yolks
- 1 teaspoon vanilla extract
- 1/2 cup butter tart filling (see below)
- 1/2 cup chopped pecans or walnuts (optional)

For the butter tart filling:

- 1/2 cup brown sugar
- 1/4 cup maple syrup
- 1/4 cup melted butter
- 1 large egg
- 1 teaspoon vanilla extract

Instructions:

1. Make the butter tart filling:
    - In a bowl, whisk together the brown sugar, maple syrup, melted butter, egg, and vanilla extract until smooth. Set aside.
2. Prepare the ice cream base:
    - In a saucepan, combine the heavy cream, whole milk, and brown sugar. Heat over medium heat, stirring occasionally, until the mixture is hot but not boiling.
    - In a separate bowl, whisk the egg yolks until smooth. Gradually whisk in about 1/2 cup of the hot cream mixture to temper the eggs.
    - Pour the tempered egg mixture back into the saucepan with the remaining cream mixture, whisking constantly.
    - Cook the mixture over medium heat, stirring constantly, until it thickens enough to coat the back of a spoon, about 5-7 minutes. Do not let it boil.
    - Remove the saucepan from the heat and stir in the vanilla extract. Let the mixture cool to room temperature.
3. Churn the ice cream:
    - Once the ice cream base has cooled, churn it in an ice cream maker according to the manufacturer's instructions.

- During the last few minutes of churning, add the butter tart filling and chopped pecans or walnuts, if using, and continue churning until well combined.
4. Freeze the ice cream:
    - Transfer the churned ice cream to a freezer-safe container. Press a piece of parchment paper or plastic wrap directly onto the surface of the ice cream to prevent ice crystals from forming.
    - Freeze the ice cream for at least 4 hours, or until firm.
5. Serve:
    - Scoop the butter tart ice cream into bowls or cones and enjoy!

This butter tart ice cream is a delightful treat on its own, but you can also serve it with additional butter tart filling drizzled on top for an extra indulgent experience. Enjoy!

Canadian whisky cocktails

Whisky Sour:

- 2 oz Canadian whisky
- 3/4 oz fresh lemon juice
- 1/2 oz simple syrup
- Ice
- Lemon wheel, for garnish
- Maraschino cherry, for garnishInstructions:
    - In a shaker, combine the Canadian whisky, fresh lemon juice, and simple syrup.
    - Fill the shaker with ice and shake well until chilled.
    - Strain the mixture into a rocks glass filled with ice.
    - Garnish with a lemon wheel and a maraschino cherry.

2. Maple Old Fashioned:

- 2 oz Canadian whisky
- 1/4 oz maple syrup
- 2 dashes Angostura bitters
- Ice
- Orange peel, for garnishInstructions:
    - In a mixing glass, combine the Canadian whisky, maple syrup, and Angostura bitters.
    - Fill the glass with ice and stir well until chilled.
    - Strain the mixture into a rocks glass filled with ice.
    - Express the oils from the orange peel over the drink and garnish.

3. Canadian Caesar:

- 1 1/2 oz Canadian whisky
- 4 oz Clamato juice
- 3 dashes hot sauce
- 3 dashes Worcestershire sauce
- Pinch of celery salt
- Ice
- Celery stalk, pickled bean, or bacon strip, for garnish
- Lime wedge, for garnishInstructions:
    - Rim a highball glass with celery salt.

- Fill the glass with ice.
- Add the Canadian whisky, Clamato juice, hot sauce, Worcestershire sauce, and celery salt to the glass.
- Stir gently to combine.
- Garnish with a celery stalk, pickled bean, or bacon strip, and a lime wedge.

4. Canadian Maple Manhattan:

- 2 oz Canadian whisky
- 1/2 oz sweet vermouth
- 1/4 oz maple syrup
- 2 dashes Angostura bitters
- Ice
- Maraschino cherry, for garnishInstructions:
    - In a mixing glass, combine the Canadian whisky, sweet vermouth, maple syrup, and Angostura bitters.
    - Fill the glass with ice and stir well until chilled.
    - Strain the mixture into a chilled cocktail glass.
    - Garnish with a maraschino cherry.

Enjoy experimenting with these Canadian whisky cocktails! Adjust the ingredients to suit your taste preferences.

Quebecois sugar pie (tarte au sucre)

Ingredients:

For the pie crust:

- 1 1/4 cups all-purpose flour
- 1/2 teaspoon salt
- 1/2 cup unsalted butter, chilled and cubed
- 1/4 cup ice water

For the filling:

- 1 cup brown sugar
- 1/2 cup maple syrup
- 1/4 cup heavy cream
- 2 tablespoons all-purpose flour
- 2 tablespoons unsalted butter, melted
- 1 teaspoon vanilla extract
- Pinch of salt

Instructions:

1. Make the pie crust:
    - In a large mixing bowl, combine the flour and salt.
    - Add the chilled cubed butter and use a pastry cutter or your fingers to work the butter into the flour until the mixture resembles coarse crumbs.
    - Gradually add the ice water, a tablespoon at a time, and mix until the dough comes together.
    - Shape the dough into a disk, wrap it in plastic wrap, and refrigerate for at least 30 minutes.
2. Preheat the oven:
    - Preheat your oven to 375°F (190°C).
3. Roll out the pie crust:
    - On a lightly floured surface, roll out the chilled pie dough into a circle large enough to fit into a 9-inch pie dish. Transfer the dough to the pie dish and trim any excess dough from the edges. Crimp the edges decoratively.
4. Prepare the filling:
    - In a mixing bowl, combine the brown sugar, maple syrup, heavy cream, flour, melted butter, vanilla extract, and salt. Mix until smooth and well combined.

5. Assemble the pie:
   - Pour the filling mixture into the prepared pie crust, spreading it out evenly.
6. Bake the pie:
   - Place the pie in the preheated oven and bake for 45-50 minutes, or until the filling is set and the crust is golden brown.
7. Cool and serve:
   - Allow the pie to cool completely on a wire rack before serving. The filling will continue to set as it cools.
   - Serve slices of the Québécois sugar pie on its own or with a dollop of whipped cream or a scoop of vanilla ice cream, if desired.

Enjoy this indulgent Québécois sugar pie as a delightful taste of Canadian culinary tradition!

Pacific oysters Rockefeller

Ingredients:

- 12 Pacific oysters, shucked, with bottom shells reserved
- 1/2 cup unsalted butter
- 1/2 cup finely chopped shallots
- 2 cloves garlic, minced
- 1 cup fresh spinach, chopped
- 1/4 cup chopped parsley
- 1/4 cup chopped chives
- 1/4 cup breadcrumbs
- 1/4 cup grated Parmesan cheese
- Salt and pepper, to taste
- Lemon wedges, for serving
- Crushed ice, for serving

Instructions:

1. Preheat the oven: Preheat your oven to 450°F (230°C).
2. Prepare the oysters: Clean the shucked oysters and place them back in their bottom shells. Arrange the shells on a baking sheet lined with crushed ice to keep them stable.
3. Make the Rockefeller sauce:
    - In a skillet, melt the butter over medium heat.
    - Add the chopped shallots and garlic, and sauté until softened and fragrant, about 2-3 minutes.
    - Stir in the chopped spinach and cook until wilted, about 2 minutes.
    - Remove the skillet from the heat and stir in the chopped parsley and chives.
    - Season the mixture with salt and pepper to taste.
4. Assemble the oysters Rockefeller:
    - Spoon the Rockefeller sauce over each oyster in its shell, covering it generously.
    - In a small bowl, mix together the breadcrumbs and grated Parmesan cheese. Sprinkle this mixture over the top of each oyster.
5. Bake the oysters:
    - Place the baking sheet with the assembled oysters in the preheated oven.
    - Bake for 8-10 minutes, or until the topping is golden brown and the oysters are heated through.

6. Serve:
    - Carefully transfer the baked oysters Rockefeller to a serving platter.
    - Serve hot, garnished with lemon wedges on the side.

Enjoy these Pacific Oysters Rockefeller as a decadent appetizer or as part of a seafood feast!

Prairie oysters (bull testicles)

Ingredients:

- 4 bull testicles (also known as calf fries)
- 1 cup all-purpose flour
- Salt and pepper, to taste
- Vegetable oil, for frying
- Hot sauce or salsa, for serving (optional)

Instructions:

1. Prepare the bull testicles:
    - Rinse the bull testicles under cold water and pat them dry with paper towels.
    - Using a sharp knife, carefully remove the tough outer membrane from each testicle.
    - Slice the testicles into thin slices, about 1/4 inch thick.
2. Coat the slices:
    - In a shallow bowl, combine the all-purpose flour with salt and pepper to taste.
    - Dredge the bull testicle slices in the seasoned flour, shaking off any excess.
3. Fry the prairie oysters:
    - Heat vegetable oil in a deep fryer or large skillet to 350°F (175°C).
    - Carefully add the coated bull testicle slices to the hot oil in batches, making sure not to overcrowd the pan.
    - Fry the slices for 2-3 minutes, or until golden brown and crispy.
    - Using a slotted spoon, transfer the fried prairie oysters to a plate lined with paper towels to drain excess oil.
4. Serve:
    - Serve the prairie oysters hot, with your choice of dipping sauce such as hot sauce or salsa on the side.

Enjoy this unique delicacy with a sense of culinary adventure! Keep in mind that prairie oysters have a distinctive flavor and texture, so they may not be for everyone.

Maple-glazed pork chops

Ingredients:

- 4 bone-in pork chops, about 3/4 inch thick
- Salt and pepper, to taste
- 2 tablespoons olive oil
- 1/4 cup maple syrup
- 2 tablespoons Dijon mustard
- 2 cloves garlic, minced
- 1 teaspoon fresh thyme leaves (or 1/2 teaspoon dried thyme)
- 1/2 teaspoon smoked paprika (optional)
- Chopped fresh parsley, for garnish (optional)

Instructions:

1. Prepare the pork chops:
    - Pat the pork chops dry with paper towels and season them generously with salt and pepper on both sides.
2. Make the glaze:
    - In a small bowl, whisk together the maple syrup, Dijon mustard, minced garlic, thyme leaves, and smoked paprika (if using) until well combined.
3. Cook the pork chops:
    - Heat the olive oil in a large skillet over medium-high heat.
    - Once the skillet is hot, add the pork chops and cook for 3-4 minutes on each side, or until they are golden brown and cooked through. The internal temperature should reach 145°F (63°C).
    - During the last minute of cooking, pour the maple glaze over the pork chops in the skillet, allowing it to coat the chops evenly. Let the glaze cook for about 1 minute, until it thickens slightly and caramelizes.
    - Flip the pork chops once more to coat them in the glaze.
4. Serve:
    - Transfer the glazed pork chops to a serving platter.
    - Garnish with chopped fresh parsley, if desired.
    - Serve hot, with any remaining glaze drizzled over the top.

These maple-glazed pork chops pair well with a variety of sides, such as roasted vegetables, mashed potatoes, or a simple green salad. Enjoy the delicious combination of savory pork and sweet maple glaze!

Atlantic salmon burgers

Ingredients:

- 1 pound fresh Atlantic salmon, skin removed and diced
- 1/4 cup breadcrumbs
- 1/4 cup finely chopped red onion
- 2 cloves garlic, minced
- 1 tablespoon Dijon mustard
- 1 tablespoon mayonnaise
- 1 tablespoon lemon juice
- 1 teaspoon lemon zest
- 1 tablespoon chopped fresh dill (or 1 teaspoon dried dill)
- Salt and pepper, to taste
- 1 tablespoon olive oil
- Burger buns
- Lettuce, tomato, onion, and other desired toppings

Instructions:

1. Prepare the salmon mixture:
    - In a food processor, pulse the diced salmon until it is finely chopped but still has some texture.
    - Transfer the chopped salmon to a mixing bowl and add the breadcrumbs, chopped red onion, minced garlic, Dijon mustard, mayonnaise, lemon juice, lemon zest, and chopped dill.
    - Season with salt and pepper to taste.
    - Mix everything together until well combined.
2. Form the salmon patties:
    - Divide the salmon mixture into 4 equal portions.
    - Shape each portion into a patty about 1/2 inch thick, pressing firmly to hold the shape.
3. Cook the salmon burgers:
    - Heat the olive oil in a skillet over medium heat.
    - Once the skillet is hot, add the salmon patties and cook for about 4-5 minutes on each side, or until they are cooked through and golden brown on the outside.
4. Assemble the burgers:
    - Toast the burger buns if desired.
    - Place a salmon patty on the bottom half of each bun.

        - Add lettuce, tomato, onion, and any other desired toppings.
        - Place the top half of the bun on top of each burger.
   5. Serve:
        - Serve the Atlantic salmon burgers immediately, with your favorite sides such as sweet potato fries, coleslaw, or a green salad.

Enjoy these delicious and flavorful Atlantic salmon burgers as a healthier alternative to traditional beef burgers!

Moose stew

Ingredients:

- 2 pounds moose meat, cut into 1-inch cubes
- 2 tablespoons all-purpose flour
- Salt and pepper, to taste
- 2 tablespoons vegetable oil
- 1 onion, chopped
- 2 cloves garlic, minced
- 4 carrots, peeled and chopped
- 2 stalks celery, chopped
- 4 potatoes, peeled and diced
- 4 cups beef or vegetable broth
- 2 bay leaves
- 1 teaspoon dried thyme
- 1 teaspoon dried rosemary
- Chopped fresh parsley, for garnish (optional)

Instructions:

1. Coat the moose meat:
    - In a bowl, combine the cubed moose meat with the all-purpose flour, salt, and pepper. Toss to coat the meat evenly.
2. Brown the moose meat:
    - Heat the vegetable oil in a large Dutch oven or heavy-bottomed pot over medium-high heat.
    - Once the oil is hot, add the coated moose meat in batches, making sure not to overcrowd the pot. Brown the meat on all sides, then transfer it to a plate and set aside.
3. Sauté the vegetables:
    - In the same pot, add the chopped onion and garlic. Sauté for 2-3 minutes until fragrant.
    - Add the chopped carrots, celery, and diced potatoes to the pot. Sauté for another 5 minutes, stirring occasionally.
4. Combine the ingredients:
    - Return the browned moose meat to the pot with the sautéed vegetables.
    - Pour in the beef or vegetable broth, ensuring that the meat and vegetables are submerged.
    - Add the bay leaves, dried thyme, and dried rosemary to the pot.

5. Simmer the stew:
   - Bring the stew to a simmer over medium heat.
   - Once simmering, reduce the heat to low and cover the pot with a lid.
   - Let the stew simmer gently for 2-3 hours, stirring occasionally, until the moose meat is tender and the flavors have melded together.
6. Serve:
   - Remove the bay leaves from the stew.
   - Ladle the moose stew into bowls and garnish with chopped fresh parsley, if desired.
   - Serve hot, accompanied by crusty bread or biscuits.

Enjoy this hearty and flavorful moose stew as a comforting meal on a chilly day!

Blueberry pancakes with maple syrup

Ingredients:

- 1 cup all-purpose flour
- 2 tablespoons granulated sugar
- 1 teaspoon baking powder
- 1/2 teaspoon baking soda
- 1/4 teaspoon salt
- 1 cup buttermilk (or 1 cup milk mixed with 1 tablespoon lemon juice or white vinegar)
- 1 large egg
- 2 tablespoons unsalted butter, melted
- 1 teaspoon vanilla extract
- 1 cup fresh or frozen blueberries
- Maple syrup, for serving
- Additional butter, for serving (optional)

Instructions:

1. Prepare the batter:
    - In a large mixing bowl, whisk together the all-purpose flour, granulated sugar, baking powder, baking soda, and salt until well combined.
    - In a separate bowl, whisk together the buttermilk, egg, melted butter, and vanilla extract until smooth.
    - Pour the wet ingredients into the dry ingredients and stir until just combined. Be careful not to overmix; it's okay if the batter is slightly lumpy.
    - Gently fold in the blueberries until evenly distributed throughout the batter.
2. Cook the pancakes:
    - Heat a griddle or non-stick skillet over medium heat and lightly grease it with butter or cooking spray.
    - Pour about 1/4 cup of batter onto the griddle for each pancake, leaving space between them to spread.
    - Cook the pancakes for 2-3 minutes, or until bubbles form on the surface and the edges begin to look set.
    - Carefully flip the pancakes with a spatula and cook for an additional 1-2 minutes, or until golden brown and cooked through.
    - Repeat with the remaining batter, adjusting the heat as needed to prevent burning.
3. Serve:

- Stack the cooked pancakes on a plate.
- Serve warm, topped with maple syrup and additional butter if desired.

Enjoy these delicious blueberry pancakes with maple syrup for a delightful breakfast or brunch treat! You can also customize them by adding other toppings like whipped cream or chopped nuts if you like.

Caribou steaks

Ingredients:

- 4 caribou steaks, about 6-8 ounces each
- Salt and pepper, to taste
- 2 tablespoons olive oil or clarified butter (ghee)
- Optional marinade or seasoning of your choice (e.g., garlic, herbs, soy sauce)

Instructions:

1. Prepare the steaks:
    - If desired, you can marinate the caribou steaks for added flavor. Common marinades include garlic, herbs, soy sauce, or a mixture of olive oil and balsamic vinegar. Marinate the steaks in the refrigerator for at least 30 minutes, or overnight for best results.
    - Before cooking, remove the steaks from the refrigerator and let them come to room temperature for about 30 minutes. This ensures more even cooking.
2. Season the steaks:
    - Season the caribou steaks generously with salt and pepper on both sides. You can also add any additional seasonings or herbs at this point.
3. Preheat the cooking surface:
    - Heat a skillet, grill pan, or outdoor grill over medium-high heat. Make sure the cooking surface is hot before adding the steaks.
4. Cook the steaks:
    - Add the olive oil or clarified butter to the hot skillet or grill.
    - Carefully place the seasoned caribou steaks onto the hot cooking surface. Cook the steaks for about 3-4 minutes on each side for medium-rare, or adjust the cooking time according to your desired level of doneness. Use tongs to flip the steaks halfway through cooking.
    - Caribou is lean meat, so be careful not to overcook it, as it can become tough. Aim for medium-rare to medium doneness for the best flavor and texture.
5. Rest the steaks:
    - Once cooked to your liking, remove the caribou steaks from the heat and transfer them to a plate.
    - Allow the steaks to rest for a few minutes before serving. This allows the juices to redistribute throughout the meat, ensuring juicier and more flavorful steaks.

6. Serve:
    - Serve the caribou steaks hot, with your choice of side dishes such as roasted vegetables, mashed potatoes, or a fresh salad.

Enjoy your delicious and tender caribou steaks as a nutritious and satisfying meal!

Nanaimo bar cheesecake

Ingredients:

For the crust:

- 1 1/2 cups graham cracker crumbs
- 1/2 cup shredded coconut
- 1/2 cup chopped pecans or walnuts
- 1/2 cup unsalted butter, melted

For the cheesecake filling:

- 24 oz (3 packages) cream cheese, softened
- 1 cup granulated sugar
- 3 large eggs
- 1 teaspoon vanilla extract
- 1/2 cup sour cream

For the Nanaimo bar layer:

- 1/2 cup unsalted butter
- 1/4 cup granulated sugar
- 1/3 cup cocoa powder
- 1 large egg, beaten
- 1 3/4 cups graham cracker crumbs
- 1 cup shredded coconut
- 1/2 cup chopped pecans or walnuts
- 1 teaspoon vanilla extract

For the chocolate ganache topping:

- 4 oz semi-sweet chocolate, chopped
- 1/2 cup heavy cream

Instructions:

1. Prepare the crust:
    - Preheat your oven to 350°F (175°C). Grease a 9-inch springform pan.
    - In a mixing bowl, combine the graham cracker crumbs, shredded coconut, chopped pecans or walnuts, and melted butter. Press the mixture into the bottom of the prepared springform pan. Bake for 10 minutes, then remove from the oven and let it cool.

2. Make the cheesecake filling:
   - In a large mixing bowl, beat the cream cheese and granulated sugar until smooth and creamy.
   - Add the eggs one at a time, beating well after each addition.
   - Stir in the vanilla extract and sour cream until well combined.
   - Pour the cheesecake filling over the cooled crust in the springform pan. Smooth the top with a spatula.
3. Prepare the Nanaimo bar layer:
   - In a saucepan, melt the butter over low heat. Stir in the granulated sugar and cocoa powder until smooth.
   - Gradually add the beaten egg, stirring continuously until the mixture thickens slightly.
   - Remove the saucepan from the heat and stir in the graham cracker crumbs, shredded coconut, chopped pecans or walnuts, and vanilla extract until well combined.
   - Spread the Nanaimo bar mixture evenly over the cheesecake filling in the springform pan.
4. Bake the cheesecake:
   - Bake the cheesecake in the preheated oven for 45-50 minutes, or until the center is set and the edges are lightly golden.
   - Remove the cheesecake from the oven and let it cool completely in the pan on a wire rack.
5. Make the chocolate ganache topping:
   - In a heatproof bowl, combine the chopped semi-sweet chocolate and heavy cream.
   - Microwave the mixture in 30-second intervals, stirring after each interval, until the chocolate is melted and the ganache is smooth.
6. Finish and chill:
   - Pour the chocolate ganache over the cooled cheesecake, spreading it evenly over the top.
   - Refrigerate the cheesecake for at least 4 hours, or until set.
7. Serve:
   - Once chilled and set, remove the cheesecake from the springform pan and slice into portions.
   - Serve the Nanaimo bar cheesecake chilled, and enjoy!

This Nanaimo bar cheesecake is a rich and indulgent dessert that combines the best of both worlds. Enjoy each creamy, chocolatey bite!